An Ode to Hidden Corners and Cultural Resonance

ATHENS
Travel Guide
2025

INKSPIRE

Copyright

Disclaimer

The author and publisher have made every effort to ensure the accuracy and completeness of the information contained in this book. However, they assume no responsibility for errors, inaccuracies, omissions, or any other inconsistencies herein.

This book is not intended to provide legal, financial, or other professional advice.

About Our Authors

Jeremy Johnson is an acclaimed author in the world of travel writing, celebrated for his vivid and immersive narratives. With a deep curiosity and a gift for storytelling, he brings destinations to life by capturing their true essence and hidden soul. Far more than just a source of tips, his guidebooks inspire mindful exploration and a genuine respect for cultural richness. Whether you're a globe-trotting adventurer or a weekend wanderer, Jeremy's work invites you to travel deeper and connect more meaningfully with the world around you.

Gary Saint is an award-winning travel writer and photographer whose journeys have spanned over 60 countries across six continents during his rich, decade-long career. Known for his vivid storytelling and adventurous spirit, Gary crafts narratives that go far beyond typical travel advice. His work artfully combines useful insights with captivating experiences, all while highlighting his deep admiration for the world's cultures and landscapes. A strong believer in travel as a force for good, Gary's guides encourage readers—from seasoned globetrotters to curious newcomers—to explore with purpose and embrace the wonders of our planet.

ATHENS

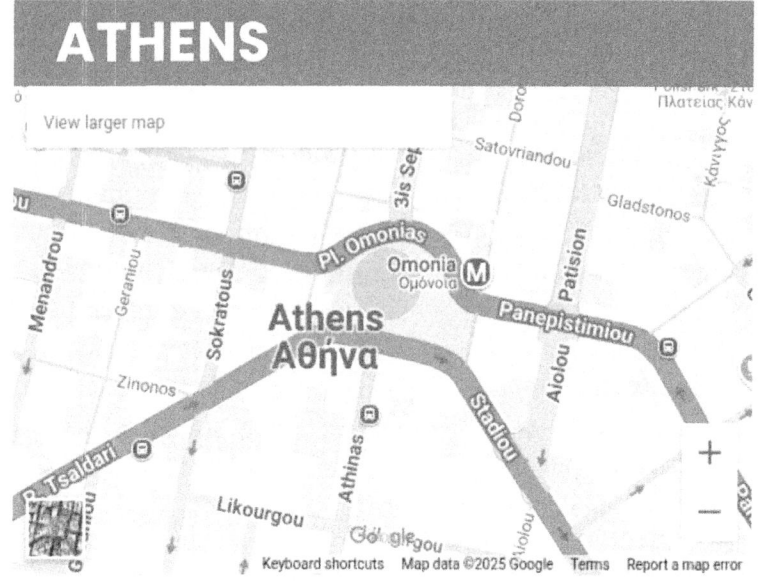

SCAN THE QR CODE

- Open your phone's camera app
- Most smartphones have a built-in QR scanner in the camera.
- Point the camera at the QR code
- Make sure the code is clear and within the frame.
- Wait for the notification
- A link or message should pop up on your screen.
- Tap the notification
- This will open the link or content in your browser or a relevant app.
- Follow the instructions on the screen
- You will be taken to a Google Maps, app where you can now click on your current location to get to your destination.

Table of Content

Introduction

Stepping off the plane at Athens International Airport, I felt a surge of anticipation ripple through me. The warm Mediterranean sun greeted my skin as I breathed in the crisp, salt-kissed air—a stark contrast to the hum of the bustling airport around me. The moment my feet touched Greek soil, the city's magnetic energy was palpable, as if history itself was whispering its secrets directly to me. I was no longer just a visitor; I was a traveler on the cusp of discovery, ready to unravel a tapestry woven from millennia of myth, culture, and vibrant life.

As I made my way through the city's streets later that day, the ancient and the modern collided with an effortless grace that caught me off guard. Around every corner, Athens revealed itself in layers: a weathered stone wall kissed by time, a lively café where locals debated politics over thick coffee, children chasing pigeons in sun-dappled plazas, and the towering silhouette of the Acropolis standing watch over it all like an eternal guardian. The city's pulse was alive—at once chaotic and serene, loud and intimate, ancient yet undeniably contemporary.

My first encounter with the Acropolis was nothing short of breathtaking. As I approached the foot of the hill, the sun was dipping low, casting a golden glow that made the Parthenon's marble columns shimmer like a beacon from the past. I found myself caught between awe and humility, overwhelmed by the sheer magnitude of what humanity had built so long ago. Here was a place where gods and mortals once intersected—a monument not just of stone, but of spirit and ambition. The whispers of history seemed to echo beneath my feet, urging me to listen closely and to learn more.

But Athens is not merely a city of relics; it's a living mosaic of cultures, flavors, and stories that unfold with every step. From vibrant street art to quiet corners where age-old traditions still thrive, the city beckons travelers to explore beyond the obvious. It invites you to taste its sun-ripened olives, savor the tang of fresh feta, and linger over late-night conversations fueled by ouzo and laughter. The city's charm is found in these moments—in the unhurried strolls through narrow alleys and the unexpected encounters with locals who embody the warmth and resilience of Greek culture.

Welcome to Athens

There's something undeniably magnetic about Athens—a city where ancient history and vibrant modern life collide in a way that few places in the world can match. Standing at the crossroads of civilizations, Athens is more than just the birthplace of democracy or home to iconic ruins; it's a living, breathing metropolis that invites every traveler to step beyond the postcards and dive into its rich, layered soul. Whether you're a history buff, a food lover, an art enthusiast, or someone simply drawn to the pulse of an extraordinary city, Athens in 2025 offers an experience that is both timeless and thrillingly new.

As you embark on this journey through Athens, you'll discover a city that is constantly evolving yet rooted in traditions that stretch back thousands of years. The year 2025 brings with it fresh energy and new stories—renewed urban spaces, innovative cultural festivals, and a growing community of locals and visitors who are shaping Athens into a destination that honors its past while embracing the future. This guide will be your companion through all of it, helping you uncover not only the famous landmarks but also the hidden gems, the neighborhood secrets, and the everyday moments that make Athens truly unforgettable.

Why Athens in 2025?

The question might seem simple: why choose Athens right now? But the answer reveals itself in layers, much like the city itself.

Athens has always been a crossroads—of people, ideas, and cultures. In 2025, this dynamic city is striking a remarkable balance between preserving its extraordinary heritage and embracing innovation. The urban landscape is transforming with thoughtful restoration projects that breathe new life into ancient sites while sustainable initiatives are reshaping the city's green spaces, public transport, and local markets. This is a city where history doesn't sit frozen in time; instead, it actively informs how Athens moves forward.

In recent years, Athens has become a hub for creative expression and entrepreneurship. Artists, chefs, and designers flock here, drawn by the city's unique blend of inspiration and opportunity. The neighborhoods pulse with energy—street art murals tell stories of resilience and hope, rooftop bars buzz with eclectic music, and small galleries showcase cutting-edge work alongside traditional crafts. Athens is evolving, and 2025 is shaping up to be a defining year for experiencing this vibrant renaissance firsthand.

Moreover, the city's culinary scene has blossomed into an enticing journey of its own. The ancient Greek diet—rich in olive oil, fresh vegetables, seafood, and herbs—meets contemporary creativity in a way that tantalizes every palate. Traditional tavernas stand shoulder to shoulder with modern eateries, vegan and vegetarian options abound, and food markets hum with life, offering fresh, locally sourced ingredients and artisanal products. Eating in Athens in 2025 is a celebration of flavor and heritage.

Finally, Athens is welcoming more visitors than ever, but thanks to thoughtful tourism planning, the experience remains authentic and accessible. New pedestrian zones, improved public transport, and guided walking routes help travelers explore comfortably while minimizing their footprint. Local initiatives encourage visitors to engage respectfully with the culture and environment, fostering meaningful connections rather than fleeting encounters. In 2025, Athens is inviting you not just to see the city, but to be part of its story.

Top Reasons to Visit

If you're wondering what sets Athens apart in a world full of remarkable destinations, here are some of the top reasons why 2025 is the perfect time to visit:

1. Unrivaled Historical Depth

Athens is a city where history breathes on every street corner. From the majestic Acropolis overlooking the city to lesser-known archaeological sites scattered throughout neighborhoods, the layers of history invite exploration. The city isn't a museum frozen in time—it's a place where ancient ruins coexist with bustling cafes, allowing visitors to feel the past in the present moment.

2. A Thriving Cultural Scene

Beyond its ancient monuments, Athens is a vibrant center for arts and culture. The city hosts an array of festivals throughout the year, including music, film, theater, and dance. Contemporary art galleries and museums spotlight both Greek talent and international names, while traditional crafts continue to flourish in local workshops.

3. Culinary Adventures

Food in Athens is a journey through tradition and innovation. Sample classic Greek dishes in family-run tavernas or indulge in inventive cuisine at cutting-edge restaurants. Seasonal markets offer fresh produce, cheeses, and olives that bring the Mediterranean diet to life. Whatever your taste, Athens offers flavors that linger long after the last bite.

4. Warm and Welcoming Locals

Greek hospitality is legendary, and Athens exemplifies it in every encounter. Locals are eager to share their city's stories and traditions, whether through a conversation over coffee or an invitation to a neighborhood festival. This warmth turns a trip into a deeply personal experience.

5. Scenic Neighborhoods and Urban Vibes

From the cobblestone charm of Plaka to the trendy streets of Exarchia, Athens' neighborhoods each have their own character and pace. You can wander through leafy parks, relax on a rooftop with panoramic views, or dive into bustling markets. The diversity of urban life here ensures every visitor finds a corner that feels like home.

6. Strategic Location for Exploration

Athens is also the gateway to a wealth of nearby treasures. With easy access to the Aegean Sea and islands like Hydra, Aegina, and Spetses, as well as day trips to Delphi and Cape Sounion, Athens serves as a perfect base for expanding your Greek adventure.

7. Sustainable and Thoughtful Tourism

In 2025, Athens is embracing responsible travel. Efforts to preserve historic sites, promote eco-friendly transport, and support local businesses create a tourism experience that respects the city's heritage and environment. Visitors are encouraged to engage in ways that leave a positive impact.

How to Use This Guide

This guide is designed to be both comprehensive and flexible, tailored to help you navigate Athens on your own terms. Whether you're planning your first trip or returning to uncover new layers, the structure allows you to dive deep or skim the surface as you wish.

The chapters are arranged to mirror the natural flow of a visit—from your arrival and orientation to the neighborhoods, sights, dining, and cultural experiences. Each chapter includes detailed sub-sections that focus on specific areas or themes, making it easy to find the information you need. For example, if you're particularly interested in ancient history, Chapter 4 offers an in-depth look at the must-see archaeological sites, while Chapter 6 opens the door to Athens' culinary treasures.

Throughout the book, you'll find practical tips woven into the narrative—advice on transport, safety, budgeting, and etiquette—so you can travel confidently and comfortably. You'll also encounter suggestions for day trips, cultural events, and seasonal activities to help you time your visit perfectly.

One of the guiding principles behind this book is authenticity. Rather than just listing famous spots, it aims to immerse you in the everyday life of Athens, revealing the city through the eyes of locals and seasoned travelers alike. You'll learn how to balance classic must-sees with off-the-beaten-path discoveries, gaining a richer, more personal experience.

Navigating Athens

Stepping off the plane at Athens International Airport, the city's vibrant energy is almost palpable. Whether it's your first time visiting or you're returning to this historic metropolis, knowing how to move efficiently and confidently from arrival to your chosen destination can transform your trip. Athens, a sprawling city blending the ancient with the contemporary, offers a variety of transport options designed to suit all types of travelers. From the moment you land, the options for navigating this urban tapestry are abundant, making it easy to dive right into the experience.

Athens International Airport: Arrival Tips and Transfers

Athens International Airport, officially named Eleftherios Venizelos, stands as a modern gateway to Greece's capital. Located approximately 20 kilometers east of the city center, the airport efficiently manages millions of travelers every year. Upon landing, the first priority is often navigating arrivals smoothly and choosing the best mode of transfer to your accommodation or next destination.

For those arriving after a long journey, the airport's amenities provide a welcome respite—ranging from cozy cafes to currency exchange booths and reliable Wi-Fi. As you collect your luggage and pass through customs, you'll find information desks staffed with helpful personnel ready to assist with inquiries about transportation and sightseeing.

When it comes to transfers, you have several solid choices. The metro line connects the airport directly to the heart of Athens, offering a fast and budget-friendly option that bypasses city traffic. For a more private and convenient ride, taxis are readily available outside the terminal, operating 24/7 and regulated with fixed fares depending on the destination. Alternatively, shuttle buses offer another economical way to reach popular hubs within the city, though they may take longer due to stops.

Pre-booking transfers is a smart move, especially during peak travel seasons. Many services allow you to reserve private cars or group shuttles online, providing peace of mind and streamlined arrival. No matter your preference, Athens

International Airport's connectivity ensures your first steps into the city are smooth and hassle-free.

Public Transport Overview: Metro, Buses, and Trams

Once you've settled into the rhythm of Athens, public transportation becomes your best ally for exploring the city's diverse neighborhoods and attractions. Athens boasts a comprehensive system that includes metro lines, buses, and trams, all designed to interconnect seamlessly.

The Athens Metro, launched in the early 2000s, is both efficient and modern, rapidly becoming the backbone of the city's transit network. Currently consisting of three main lines, it links the airport, suburbs, and central districts with stops at key locations like Syntagma Square, Monastiraki, and the Acropolis. The metro is praised not only for its punctuality but also for its cleanliness and accessibility, making it a preferred choice for locals and tourists alike.

Buses fill in the gaps where the metro doesn't reach, offering an extensive web of routes across the sprawling cityscape. While bus schedules can be affected by traffic, their frequency remains high, and many lines operate late into the evening. Night buses are available, providing transport options after metro hours close, though it's advisable to check the current routes as schedules can shift.

Trams add a scenic element to public transit, running mainly along the coast and connecting the city center to southern suburbs like Glyfada and Voula. Riding the tram offers a pleasant break from the bustling city streets, with views of the sea and easy access to beachside cafés and parks.

Tickets for all public transport modes are unified, meaning a single fare covers metro, bus, and tram rides within a specified time frame, simplifying travel planning. These tickets are affordable and can be purchased at stations, kiosks, or via mobile apps, ensuring convenience at your fingertips.

Taxi, Ride-Sharing, and Bike Rentals

While public transport covers much of Athens well, taxis and ride-sharing services provide flexibility, especially for travelers with luggage, those venturing late at night, or anyone seeking direct routes to less accessible spots.

Taxis in Athens are plentiful and easy to spot, painted traditionally in yellow. The meter system is standard, but it's wise to confirm the estimated fare beforehand or request the driver to use the meter to avoid misunderstandings. During daytime, taxis can be hailed directly on the street or found at designated taxi stands near popular spots and transit hubs. At night, it's often easier and safer to book a taxi via phone or apps.

Ride-sharing has gained popularity in Athens, with services like Beat offering a convenient alternative to traditional taxis. Beat allows users to compare prices, track their driver's arrival, and pay cashless, making it a favorite among tech-savvy travelers and locals. The platform also features safety measures like driver ratings and a 24/7 support line, enhancing passenger confidence.

For those keen to explore Athens at their own pace, bike rentals are an excellent option. The city has been steadily improving its bike lanes and promoting cycling as a sustainable way to navigate urban spaces. Several rental shops in the city center and near popular tourist areas provide a range of bikes, from traditional models to electric-assisted ones, ideal for tackling Athens' hilly terrain. Cycling allows for intimate discovery, letting you pause spontaneously at markets, cafés, or viewpoints inaccessible by car or bus.

E-scooters have also entered the urban transport scene, although regulations vary, so it's important to check local rules and safety guidelines before renting.

Accessibility and Travel for Differently-Abled Visitors

Athens is steadily evolving to become more inclusive and accessible for all visitors. While the city's ancient heritage can sometimes present physical challenges, significant strides have been made to improve mobility for differently-abled travelers.

Athens International Airport is fully equipped with accessible facilities, including ramps, elevators, and reserved parking. Staff are trained to assist passengers with reduced mobility, and advanced notice can help ensure additional support is available upon arrival.

Within the city, the metro system leads the way in accessibility improvements. Most stations feature elevators, tactile paving for the visually impaired, and priority seating. Trams and modern buses also accommodate wheelchairs, though it's advisable to verify specific routes beforehand.

Many major museums, galleries, and historical sites now offer ramps, audio guides, and specialized tours designed to cater to visitors with diverse needs. The Acropolis Museum, for instance, provides accessible entrances and elevators, making it easier for all to experience the richness of Greek history.

Taxis and ride-sharing services often have vehicles adapted for wheelchair access, but advanced booking is recommended to ensure availability. Cycling and e-scooter options may be limited depending on individual mobility requirements, so it's best to plan accordingly.

Overall, while Athens retains the charm and complexity of a city shaped over millennia, the commitment to accessibility is clear and growing. Differently-abled visitors can confidently navigate Athens with a little preparation and the support of resources highlighted throughout this guide.

Athens Neighborhoods and Districts Overview

Athens is a city of vibrant contrasts, where the ancient seamlessly intertwines with the contemporary, and each neighborhood pulses with its own distinctive character. To truly appreciate Athens in 2025, one must venture beyond the iconic landmarks and immerse in the mosaic of districts that give the city its soul. Understanding the essence of these neighborhoods not only enhances your itinerary but enriches your connection with the city's living culture. As you move through Athens, each district offers a fresh perspective—whether steeped in history, buzzing with nightlife, or blossoming with creative energy.

Plaka: The Historic Heart

Plaka stands as the beating historic heart of Athens, cradled beneath the towering presence of the Acropolis. Walking through its narrow, winding streets feels like stepping back in time, where every corner tells a story etched in stone and vine-covered walls. The charm of Plaka lies in its intimate scale: cobblestone paths lined with neoclassical buildings, family-run tavernas, and quaint shops selling handmade jewelry and traditional crafts.

As dawn breaks, Plaka's peaceful aura invites quiet exploration. Small cafés open their doors, serving rich Greek coffee and freshly baked pastries. By midday, the area comes alive with tourists and locals mingling amidst the aroma of souvlaki grilling on street corners. Historical landmarks like the Roman Agora and the Tower of the Winds punctuate the neighborhood, offering glimpses into Athens' layered past.

Plaka is more than a preserved relic—it is a vibrant community where tradition meets daily life. Street musicians perform impromptu concerts, and local artists display their work in small galleries tucked away in alleyways. For anyone seeking to soak up Athens' heritage in a setting that feels personal and unhurried, Plaka is indispensable.

Monastiraki and Psiri: Markets and Nightlife

Just a short stroll from Plaka, Monastiraki and Psiri offer a contrasting energy—boisterous, eclectic, and endlessly entertaining. Monastiraki is best known for its sprawling flea market, a bustling labyrinth of stalls and vendors selling everything from antiques and vintage clothing to handmade souvenirs. The marketplace is a sensory overload, rich with colors, scents, and the lively calls of sellers vying for attention.

As afternoon fades, the mood shifts in both neighborhoods. Psiri, once an overlooked quarter, has reinvented itself as Athens' premier nightlife destination. The streets fill with young Athenians and visitors drawn to its multitude of bars, tavernas, and music venues. Here, traditional bouzouki rhythms mix with contemporary beats, creating a soundscape that reflects the city's evolving cultural fabric.

Monastiraki's rooftop bars offer breathtaking views of the Acropolis illuminated against the night sky, an unforgettable backdrop for evening drinks. Both neighborhoods thrive on their diversity, blending old-world charm with modern urban flair, making them essential stops for those looking to experience the lively pulse of Athens after dark.

Kolonaki: Sophistication and Boutiques

In stark contrast to the historic and bohemian vibes of the old town, Kolonaki presents an aura of refined sophistication. Nestled on the slopes of Mount Lycabettus, this upscale neighborhood is a magnet for fashionistas, art lovers, and gourmands. Kolonaki's streets are dotted with high-end boutiques showcasing international designers alongside elegant Greek labels, creating a stylish shopping experience that rivals Europe's fashion capitals.

Cafés spill onto sidewalks, where well-dressed locals sip espresso or enjoy leisurely lunches at chic bistros. Art galleries abound, reflecting Athens' thriving contemporary art scene, while bookshops and antique stores add to the district's intellectual allure. Kolonaki also hosts some of the city's finest museums, such as the Benaki Museum, which elegantly bridges Greece's past and present.

Evenings in Kolonaki take on a polished tone, with wine bars and gourmet restaurants offering refined tastes and ambiance. It's a place to see and be seen—a neighborhood that effortlessly blends cosmopolitan flair with Greek warmth.

Exarchia: Street Art and Alternative Culture

For those drawn to the raw, unfiltered side of Athens, Exarchia offers an immersive experience steeped in alternative culture and political history. Known as the city's anarchist quarter, Exarchia is a vibrant canvas for street art, with walls covered in murals and graffiti that range from poignant social commentary to bold artistic statements.

The neighborhood pulses with youthful energy, fueled by a network of cafés, independent bookstores, and music venues that champion underground and experimental scenes. Exarchia's roots in activism and intellectual discourse are palpable—public squares often host spirited debates, poetry readings, and impromptu performances.

Despite its reputation as a rebellious enclave, Exarchia is also a welcoming community where diversity thrives. Visitors can find cozy tavernas serving hearty Greek fare, quirky shops selling vintage records, and spaces dedicated to community gatherings. Exploring Exarchia offers a glimpse into Athens' contemporary social dynamics and a chance to engage with its grassroots cultural movements.

Pangrati: Emerging Hipster Hub

Pangrati has quietly emerged as one of Athens' most exciting neighborhoods, blending residential calm with a blossoming creative scene. Once overshadowed by its flashier neighbors, this district is now gaining recognition for its hip cafés, artisanal bakeries, and boutique shops that attract a younger, trend-conscious crowd.

Pangrati's streets invite relaxed strolls amid neoclassical buildings and leafy parks, offering a more laid-back alternative to the city center's frenetic pace. Its cafes serve expertly brewed coffee alongside inventive brunch menus, while bars and small music venues have begun cultivating a reputation for quality and originality.

Artisans and designers are establishing studios and galleries here, contributing to Pangrati's growing cultural footprint. It's a neighborhood where tradition and innovation intersect gently, appealing to visitors who appreciate authenticity wrapped in a modern vibe.

Glyfada and the Athens Riviera

Stretching along the Athenian coast, Glyfada and the broader Athens Riviera present a refreshing counterpoint to the urban core. This seaside district offers sun-drenched beaches, turquoise waters, and a cosmopolitan atmosphere that draws Athenians and tourists seeking leisure and luxury.

Glyfada itself is a bustling seaside town known for its marina, upscale shops, and lively dining scene. Here, beach clubs and seafood tavernas line the waterfront, inviting visitors to savor fresh catch while watching the sunset. The area is also home to golf courses and spas, catering to those looking for relaxation and recreation.

Beyond Glyfada, the Riviera extends along the coast, dotted with charming towns like Vouliagmeni and Varkiza. The natural beauty of this stretch is striking—cliffs, pine forests, and sandy bays create a serene setting perfect for swimming, sailing, or simply unwinding.

The Riviera's accessibility from central Athens makes it an ideal day-trip destination or a tranquil retreat after days of city exploration. It embodies the Greek ideal of combining cultural richness with the pleasures of nature.

Iconic Historical and Archaeological Sites

Athens is a city where history is not just a chapter in a textbook, but a living, breathing presence felt at every step. Walking through the city, you traverse a landscape steeped in stories that have shaped Western civilization. Athens' iconic historical and archaeological sites are gateways to these stories, each monument echoing the grandeur and complexity of a past that still captivates the imagination today. In 2025, these sites are as essential as ever—vivid reminders of the city's rich heritage, yet seamlessly integrated into the rhythm of modern life.

The Acropolis and Parthenon

No visit to Athens is complete without experiencing the Acropolis, the ancient citadel that soars above the city like a timeless sentinel. From the moment you approach the hill, the sense of awe is immediate. The Parthenon, the crowning jewel of the Acropolis, stands proudly atop, its Doric columns and intricate sculptures speaking of artistic mastery and religious devotion from the 5th century BCE.

Ascending the Acropolis path, you step into a world where myth and history intertwine. The site was originally a fortress but evolved into a sacred precinct dedicated primarily to Athena, the city's patron goddess. The Parthenon itself was constructed during the golden age of Pericles, embodying ideals of democracy, beauty, and power.

Despite centuries of damage from wars, explosions, and pollution, restoration efforts have preserved the monument's grandeur, allowing visitors to appreciate its architectural brilliance and symbolic significance.

Beyond the Parthenon, the Acropolis complex includes other remarkable structures like the Erechtheion, famed for its Caryatid columns—sculpted female figures that appear to bear the weight of the porch with graceful strength. The Temple of Athena Nike, smaller yet exquisitely detailed, adds to the sacred atmosphere. Standing here, with panoramic views of Athens sprawling beneath, it is easy to understand why this site is often called the cradle of Western civilization.

Visiting the Acropolis in 2025 also means engaging with it in new ways. Advanced audio guides and augmented reality apps enrich the experience, allowing you to see reconstructions of the site as it once was, and hear the stories behind its creation and survival. Evening visits, when the monuments are dramatically lit against the night sky, provide a magical perspective that lingers in memory.

The Acropolis

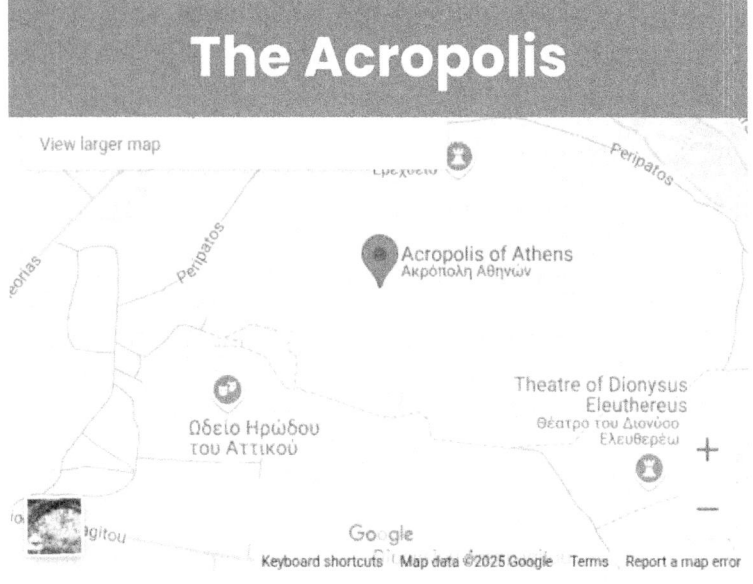

Acropolis of Athens
Ακρόπολη Αθηνών

Theatre of Dionysus
Eleuthereus
Θέατρο του Διονύσου
Ελευθερέω

Ωδείο Ηρώδου
του Αττικού

Google

Keyboard shortcuts | Map data ©2025 Google | Terms | Report a map error

SCAN THE QR CODE

- Open your phone's camera app
- Most smartphones have a built-in QR scanner in the camera.
- Point the camera at the QR code
- Make sure the code is clear and within the frame.
- Wait for the notification
- A link or message should pop up on your screen.
- Tap the notification
- This will open the link or content in your browser or a relevant app.
- Follow the instructions on the screen
- You will be taken to a Google Maps, app where you can now click on your current location to get to your destination.

The Ancient Agora

Just northwest of the Acropolis lies the Ancient Agora, a sprawling archaeological site that was once the vibrant heart of public life in Athens. Far from being just a marketplace, the Agora was the center of political debate, philosophy, and social interaction, embodying the democratic spirit Athens is famous for.

Walking through the ruins, you encounter remnants of stoas (covered walkways), temples, and administrative buildings that hosted everything from assemblies to courts. The well-preserved Hephaisteion, often called the Temple of Hephaestus, is a highlight—an elegant Doric temple dedicated to the god of craftsmanship, standing almost intact and overlooking the Agora's grounds.

The Agora's Museum, housed in the reconstructed Stoa of Attalos, offers a rich collection of artifacts unearthed from the site, including pottery, coins, and inscriptions that illuminate everyday life in ancient Athens. Exploring the museum after wandering the ruins helps bridge the gap between past and present, bringing the Agora's history to life.

For those interested in philosophy, the Agora is also where Socrates once walked and debated, challenging Athenians to question their beliefs and values. It is this intellectual legacy that makes the Ancient Agora much more than ruins—it is a symbol of inquiry and civic engagement that resonates through the ages.

The Temple of Olympian Zeus

Standing in stark contrast to the smaller, more refined temples scattered throughout Athens, the Temple of Olympian Zeus impresses visitors with its monumental scale and ambition. Construction of this temple began in the 6th century BCE but was only completed nearly 700 years later under Roman Emperor Hadrian, a fact that reflects the political and cultural shifts that shaped Athens over the centuries.

Though only a fraction of the original temple remains—fifteen massive Corinthian columns still stand, their fluted shafts and ornate capitals towering over the surrounding park—the sheer size and craftsmanship speak volumes about the grandeur the temple once possessed. Dedicated to Zeus, king of the gods, the temple symbolized the power and glory of Athens, especially during the Roman period.

Visiting the Temple of Olympian Zeus offers a unique perspective on Athens' layered history. Just steps away, Hadrian's Arch marks the boundary between the ancient city and the Roman additions, a physical reminder of the city's evolving identity. The site's proximity to the National Garden and Zappeion Hall also means visitors can combine history with relaxation in verdant surroundings.

The National Archaeological Museum

For those seeking to delve deeper into Greece's ancient past, the National Archaeological Museum is an indispensable destination. As the largest archaeological museum in Greece and one of the most important worldwide, it houses a staggering collection that spans from prehistory through late antiquity.

The museum's halls are arranged to take visitors on a chronological journey through Greek civilization, displaying artifacts that range from delicate Cycladic figurines to imposing Mycenaean weapons and intricate pottery. Masterpieces such as the Mask of Agamemnon, the Antikythera Mechanism fragments, and the bronze statue of Poseidon or Zeus showcase the artistic and technological achievements of ancient Greece.

Beyond its impressive exhibits, the museum serves as a hub for archaeological research and preservation, ensuring that the treasures of Greece remain accessible to both scholars and the public. In 2025, the museum continues to innovate, offering interactive displays, virtual tours, and special exhibitions that highlight ongoing discoveries and the stories behind the artifacts.

Spending several hours here enriches any trip to Athens, providing context and depth to the ruins seen elsewhere in the city. It is a place where history is not just viewed, but understood and appreciated in its full complexity.

Kerameikos Cemetery and Archaeological Site

Often overlooked by tourists rushing to the more famous landmarks, the Kerameikos archaeological site offers a fascinating glimpse into ancient Athenian life and death. Once the city's main cemetery and a vital religious area, Kerameikos reveals the rituals and customs surrounding death, as well as insights into the city's social hierarchy.

Walking through the site, you encounter impressive funerary monuments, elaborate grave stelae, and remnants of city walls that once protected Athens. The site also includes the Sacred Gate, through which processions would have passed during important religious festivals, adding a ceremonial dimension to the experience.

Kerameikos is uniquely evocative because it connects visitors with the personal side of ancient Athens—the lives and deaths of its citizens. The small but informative museum displays artifacts found on-site, including pottery, inscriptions, and grave goods, enriching understanding of Athenian burial practices.

As a quieter, more contemplative space, Kerameikos offers a welcome respite from the crowds and a chance to reflect on the city's past in a setting that feels both intimate and profound. It is a reminder that Athens' history is not just monumental but deeply human.

Art, Museums, and Cultural Experiences

Athens is often celebrated for its ancient wonders, but its cultural heartbeat pulses strongly in the vibrant world of art, museums, and contemporary creativity. In 2025, the city stands as a dynamic hub where history and modern expression meet, offering visitors a rich tapestry of artistic experiences that extend far beyond the ruins. From world-class museums preserving millennia-old treasures to innovative galleries and thriving street art scenes, Athens invites you to immerse yourself in its multifaceted cultural landscape.

Benaki Museum

The Benaki Museum is an essential starting point for anyone seeking a comprehensive understanding of Greek culture through the ages. Housed in a magnificent neoclassical building in central Athens, this museum transcends simple categorization. Its collections span ancient artifacts, Byzantine icons, Ottoman-era treasures, and even contemporary Greek art, creating a panoramic view of the nation's artistic and historical journey.

Walking through the Benaki, you move seamlessly from one era to another. Its exhibits of classical antiquities reveal exquisite jewelry, pottery, and sculptures that highlight Greece's rich ancient heritage. Yet the museum also shines a light on lesser-known periods such as the Byzantine era, showcasing stunning religious art that emphasizes spiritual and aesthetic depth.

The museum's commitment to modern and contemporary art ensures it remains relevant and engaging. Temporary exhibitions often feature emerging Greek artists or international talents, connecting the past with present-day cultural dialogues. For travelers interested in exploring Greece's evolving identity, the Benaki offers an insightful and inspiring experience that goes beyond the familiar.

Museum of Cycladic Art

Nestled in the heart of Athens, the Museum of Cycladic Art is a treasure trove dedicated to the mysterious and elegant art of the Cycladic islands, which flourished during the Bronze Age. The museum's minimalist design complements the stark beauty of the Cycladic figurines, characterized by their simple, abstract shapes that have fascinated artists and scholars alike.

Stepping inside, visitors encounter these timeless marble figures, whose purity of form has influenced modern art and design worldwide. The museum not only displays these iconic sculptures but also contextualizes them within the broader archaeological and cultural landscape of the Aegean.

Beyond Cycladic art, the museum hosts collections of ancient Greek pottery and artifacts from the wider Mediterranean, emphasizing cross-cultural connections in antiquity. This blend of focus and breadth makes the museum a must-visit for those intrigued by the origins of artistic abstraction and the deep roots of Greek civilization.

Contemporary Art Spaces and Galleries

Athens' contemporary art scene is flourishing, marked by innovative spaces and galleries that challenge conventions and foster creativity. Districts like Metaxourgeio and Kerameikos have become vibrant art quarters, where former industrial buildings have been transformed into cutting-edge galleries and artist studios.

These spaces showcase a wide spectrum of work, from avant-garde installations to experimental multimedia projects, reflecting both local issues and global trends. The city's artists often engage with themes of identity, history, and social change, making contemporary art in Athens a lively conversation between the past and present.

Institutions such as the National Museum of Contemporary Art (EMST) play a pivotal role in promoting Greek and international artists, offering exhibitions that push boundaries and invite reflection. Smaller galleries scattered throughout the city also contribute to this thriving ecosystem, providing platforms for emerging talents and fostering artistic dialogue.

For visitors, exploring these venues offers an exciting glimpse into Athens' creative future, balancing the reverence for heritage with bold new expressions.

Cultural Festivals and Performances

Athens in 2025 buzzes with cultural festivals that celebrate its artistic diversity and bring the city's vibrant spirit to life. These events are not just entertainment; they are immersive experiences that connect audiences with the living culture of Greece.

The Athens and Epidaurus Festival, held annually during the summer, is a highlight, offering performances that range from ancient Greek drama staged in historic theaters to contemporary dance, music, and opera. Attending a play at the Odeon of Herodes Atticus, with the Acropolis as a backdrop, is an unforgettable experience that blends past and present in a breathtaking setting.

Other festivals throughout the year celebrate film, jazz, and folk traditions, while neighborhood events bring music, food, and art to local streets, creating a festive atmosphere accessible to all. These gatherings foster community, showcase artistic talents, and offer visitors an authentic taste of Athenian life beyond the usual tourist paths.

Whether it's a large-scale production or an intimate concert in a hidden courtyard, the city's cultural calendar invites exploration and engagement, making any visit to Athens rich with creative encounters.

Street Art and Urban Creativity

Athens has earned a reputation as one of Europe's street art capitals, where urban creativity transforms walls, alleys, and forgotten spaces into vibrant canvases. The city's street art scene is diverse, ranging from politically charged murals and social commentary to colorful abstractions and playful characters.

Walking through neighborhoods like Exarchia and Psiri, you encounter a living gallery where each piece tells a story—sometimes provocative, sometimes celebratory, always expressive. This form of art reflects the city's complex social and political landscape, offering insights into contemporary issues and local perspectives.

Street art tours have become popular, guiding visitors through these dynamic areas and explaining the meanings and techniques behind key works. This accessibility turns the city itself into an open-air museum, where the boundaries between art and everyday life blur.

Beyond murals, Athens fosters urban creativity through initiatives that promote community art projects, workshops, and public installations. This grassroots energy complements the city's formal cultural institutions, highlighting a vibrant dialogue between tradition and innovation.

Culinary Athens

Stepping into Athens is not just a feast for the eyes but a journey of the senses, and nowhere is this more evident than in its vibrant culinary scene. From bustling local markets where fresh produce and fragrant spices fill the air, to the time-honored taverns serving up comforting, hearty dishes, Athens offers a culinary adventure deeply rooted in tradition yet boldly embracing innovation. The city's food culture reflects its rich history, Mediterranean climate, and a modern cosmopolitan flair that makes dining here a celebration of both past and present.

Local Markets: Varvakios Agora and Central Market

At the heart of Athens' gastronomic life lies the Varvakios Agora, the Central Market, a sensory playground for any food lover. Located on Athinas Street in the city center, this market has been the culinary soul of Athens for generations, offering a vivid glimpse into the everyday life of locals.

Walking through the market's corridors, you're surrounded by vibrant stalls overflowing with fresh fruits, vegetables, aromatic herbs, and an impressive array of seafood caught from the Aegean Sea. The sounds of vendors calling out prices, the chatter of shoppers, and the clatter of knives preparing cuts of meat create a lively atmosphere that is both chaotic and inviting.

The market's meat and fish sections boast some of the freshest selections in the city. Fishmongers expertly fillet their catch of the day while butchers offer traditional Greek cuts like lamb chops, pork souvlaki skewers, and sausages. The variety is astonishing, from everyday staples to specialty items that hint at recipes passed down through centuries.

Varvakios Agora is more than just a place to shop—it's where you witness the rhythms of Greek food culture firsthand. Many locals come here daily, selecting ingredients for their meals, ensuring that freshness and quality are never compromised. Visitors can also find small eateries within the market where dishes like grilled octopus or fried calamari are served, allowing you to taste the market's offerings on the spot, often accompanied by a glass of ouzo or local wine.

Traditional Greek Taverns and Mezedopoleia

A short stroll away from the market, the streets of Athens are dotted with traditional taverns and mezedopoleia—small plates restaurants that celebrate Greek hospitality and conviviality. These establishments invite you to slow down and savor the essence of Greek cuisine: simplicity, freshness, and generosity.

In a typical taverna, wooden tables and checkered tablecloths set a cozy, welcoming scene. The menu often reads like a love letter to local ingredients and culinary customs, featuring dishes that have stood the test of time. Think moussaka layered with tender eggplant and rich béchamel, souvlaki with perfectly grilled meat skewers, and gemista—vegetables stuffed with herbed rice and baked to perfection.

Mezedopoleia add another dimension to the dining experience by focusing on meze—an array of small, flavorful plates meant to be shared. Here you'll find tzatziki, creamy yogurt mixed with cucumber and garlic; dolmades, vine leaves stuffed with rice and herbs; and saganaki, cheese fried until golden and served with a squeeze of lemon. These dishes encourage conversation and connection, as friends and family pass plates around, savoring a mosaic of tastes.

What makes these taverns special is not just the food but the atmosphere—a sense of timelessness and authenticity. Many are family-run, with recipes and traditions handed down through generations, preserving a slice of Greek culinary heritage in every bite.

Modern Greek Cuisine and Innovative Dining

While tradition anchors Athens' food scene, the city is also a playground for modern Greek cuisine that pushes boundaries and reimagines classics with contemporary techniques and global influences. Over the past decade, a new wave of chefs has emerged, blending the old with the new in inventive ways that reflect Athens' cosmopolitan character.

In neighborhoods like Kolonaki and Gazi, sleek restaurants and stylish bistros offer tasting menus that showcase seasonal ingredients sourced from Greece's diverse landscapes. Here, dishes might combine wild herbs, local cheeses, and

Mediterranean seafood with unexpected pairings or avant-garde presentations. Think slow-cooked lamb shoulder infused with aromatic herbs served alongside a puree of ancient grains, or sea bass ceviche flavored with citrus and a hint of local honey.

These modern eateries place a strong emphasis on sustainability and provenance, celebrating the story behind each ingredient. Many collaborate directly with farmers, fishermen, and artisanal producers, ensuring that their menus are a reflection of Greece's culinary bounty and a commitment to quality.

Dining in this scene is as much about artistry and discovery as it is about flavor, with chefs often presenting multi-course meals that guide you through a journey of taste and texture, each dish telling its own story.

Coffee Culture and Cafés to Know

No visit to Athens is complete without immersing yourself in its thriving coffee culture. The city pulses with a café scene that ranges from traditional coffee shops where time seems to slow, to hip, contemporary spots that blend local customs with international trends.

The Greek coffee, strong and thick, served in small cups accompanied by a glass of cold water, is a ritual deeply embedded in daily life. It's a moment of pause, a chance to connect with friends, or simply watch the city's rhythm unfold. Many cafés pride themselves on their mastery of this brew, perfecting the foam and bitterness that define the experience.

Alongside traditional coffee houses, specialty coffee shops have surged in popularity, offering expertly crafted espresso drinks, pour-overs, and cold brews made from ethically sourced beans. These cafés often feature minimalist interiors, artful presentations, and an inviting atmosphere where locals and travelers alike linger over their cups.

Neighborhoods such as Exarchia and Psiri are especially known for their eclectic mix of cafés, where you can find anything from a classic frappe—a refreshing iced coffee favored by many Athenians—to innovative blends and seasonal specials. Paired with Greek pastries like bougatsa (a custard-filled phyllo pastry) or koulouri (sesame bread rings), coffee becomes a sensory delight.

Vegan and Vegetarian Dining Options

Athens has rapidly embraced plant-based cuisine, catering to the growing number of vegan and vegetarian travelers and locals alike. The city's Mediterranean roots naturally lend themselves to this diet, with abundant fresh vegetables, legumes, and olive oil forming the basis of many dishes.

Vegan and vegetarian restaurants have flourished across the city, offering menus that highlight traditional flavors with a modern twist. These eateries often transform classics like stuffed peppers, lentil soups, and eggplant dishes into hearty, satisfying meals without animal products.

Some places specialize in creative vegan cuisine that incorporates superfoods, international spices, and innovative cooking methods. From vibrant salads bursting with local produce to rich, plant-based moussaka or souvlaki made with mushrooms or seitan, the options are diverse and flavorful.

Many traditional taverns and mezedopoleia also provide vegetarian-friendly plates, making it easy to enjoy Greek hospitality regardless of dietary preference. Seasonal vegetables grilled to perfection, fresh salads drizzled with olive oil, and homemade dips like fava (split pea puree) offer plentiful choices.

This growing trend reflects Athens' evolving culinary landscape, one that honors heritage while opening the door to inclusivity and innovation.

Athens Nightlife and Entertainment

When the sun dips below the horizon and the city lights begin to twinkle, Athens transforms into a playground of endless possibilities. Its nightlife is as diverse and dynamic as the city itself, blending ancient traditions with contemporary trends, creating an atmosphere that pulses with energy long into the early hours. Whether you seek panoramic views paired with expertly crafted cocktails, live music that stirs the soul, theatrical performances that captivate, or simply delicious street food to satisfy late-night cravings, Athens offers a rich tapestry of entertainment that never disappoints.

Rooftop Bars and Cocktail Lounges

Athens' skyline is punctuated by an ever-growing number of rooftop bars that have become iconic destinations for both locals and travelers. Perched atop historic buildings, hotels, and chic urban spots, these elevated venues offer breathtaking views of the city's landmarks—the Acropolis bathed in golden light, the sprawling urban expanse, and, on clear nights, the shimmering sea in the distance.

Walking into one of these rooftop bars, you're instantly embraced by a blend of cosmopolitan style and laid-back charm. Comfortable seating areas, mood lighting, and the gentle hum of conversation set the scene, while the bartenders craft cocktails with the precision of artists. Many places highlight Greek ingredients like mastiha liqueur, local herbs, and native citrus fruits, offering unique blends that tell a story with every sip.

Sunset is a particularly magical time here, as the sky shifts through hues of pink and purple and the city's ancient monuments glow under soft lights. Whether you prefer a classic Negroni, a refreshing mojito, or an inventive concoction infused with Mediterranean flavors, the experience of sipping a cocktail while gazing over Athens is unforgettable.

Beyond drinks, these venues often host live DJs or acoustic performances that complement the ambiance, striking a balance between sophistication and the vibrant pulse of a lively night out.

Live Music Venues and Bouzouki Clubs

For those drawn to music, Athens offers a spectrum of experiences that celebrate the city's rich cultural heritage alongside modern sounds. Central to this scene are the bouzouki clubs—venues where the unmistakable twang of the bouzouki guitar fills the air, and traditional Greek music, known as rebetiko, takes center stage.

Entering a bouzouki club is like stepping into another era. The atmosphere is intimate, with low lighting, wooden tables, and an undeniable sense of camaraderie. Patrons come not just to listen but to participate—singing along, clapping, and sometimes even dancing as the musicians pour their hearts into melodies that speak of love, loss, and the human spirit. The raw emotion and improvisational flair of these performances create a connection that transcends language.

Aside from the bouzouki, Athens' live music scene is impressively diverse. Jazz bars, indie venues, and rock clubs scatter throughout the city, each with its own vibe and loyal following. The neighborhoods of Gazi and Exarchia are particularly vibrant, hosting a variety of concerts and jam sessions that range from underground acts to internationally recognized artists.

Seasonal music festivals also bring the city alive, drawing crowds to outdoor amphitheaters and public squares. Whether it's an intimate acoustic set or a full-blown rock concert, the energy of Athens after dark is contagious, inviting everyone to lose themselves in the rhythm.

Theatrical and Cinema Experiences

Athens has long been a cradle of theater, tracing back to its origins in ancient drama. Today, the city continues this legacy with a lively theatrical scene that offers everything from classical Greek tragedies to contemporary performances.

The ancient Odeon of Herodes Atticus, located on the southern slope of the Acropolis, stands as one of the most breathtaking venues for theatrical performances. Open during the warmer months, it hosts concerts, plays, and dance shows that are enhanced by the backdrop of the illuminated Parthenon. Experiencing a performance here feels like a journey through time, where the echoes of history blend with the art of the present.

Modern theaters across the city also offer diverse programming. Small independent theaters produce avant-garde plays, experimental works, and local productions that explore social themes, while larger venues showcase musicals, ballets, and internationally acclaimed performances.

Cinema lovers are equally well catered for, with arthouse cinemas screening both Greek films and international releases. These venues often organize film festivals, retrospectives, and special screenings that celebrate cinematic art beyond the mainstream. Some outdoor cinemas operate in summer, allowing audiences to enjoy movies under the stars, often accompanied by views of iconic landmarks.

This blend of theater and film ensures that Athens' cultural calendar is full year-round, inviting visitors to engage with the city's artistic soul long after daylight fades.

Late-Night Food Spots and Street Food

After hours, Athens' culinary scene awakens in a different way, catering to night owls and revelers looking for sustenance and comfort. Late-night food spots range from casual street vendors to trendy eateries serving everything from traditional snacks to international street food inspired by global trends.

A quintessential Athenian late-night treat is the souvlaki wrap—grilled meat, fresh vegetables, and creamy tzatziki wrapped in warm pita bread. Many small shops and kiosks remain open into the early morning, offering these handheld delights to hungry partygoers. Gyros, with their savory blend of meat, tomato, onion, and fries, are another staple, embodying the perfect post-night-out fuel.

Beyond souvlaki, street food in Athens has evolved to include a diverse array of options, including vegan-friendly wraps, falafel, and even gourmet burgers. Food trucks and pop-ups frequently appear in nightlife hubs, adding variety and excitement to the scene.

For those seeking something more substantial, several late-night taverns and casual restaurants stay open late, serving traditional dishes like moussaka, grilled octopus, or fresh salads. These spots offer a warm refuge after a night of dancing or sightseeing, combining quality food with relaxed atmospheres.

Walking through the streets at night, the aroma of grilled meat, fresh herbs, and spices mingles with the buzz of conversations and laughter, creating a sensory experience that epitomizes Athens' welcoming and vibrant spirit.

Shopping in Athens

Exploring Athens offers more than just its remarkable history and vibrant culture; it also unveils a shopping scene that blends tradition, creativity, and modern style. From the bustling streets lined with souvenir shops and artisan boutiques to chic fashion districts and hidden flea markets, the city invites visitors to immerse themselves in an authentic retail experience. Whether you're hunting for unique gifts, the latest designer trends, or local delicacies like olive oil and honey, Athens has something to delight every shopper.

Souvenir Shops and Artisan Boutiques

Strolling through Athens' historic neighborhoods, you quickly notice an abundance of small shops brimming with treasures that capture the essence of Greece. These souvenir shops, often family-owned and passed down through generations, offer an array of items that celebrate the country's rich heritage. Handmade ceramics painted with intricate designs, delicate jewelry inspired by ancient motifs, and colorful textiles crafted with traditional weaving techniques are just a few examples of what you'll find.

Many artisan boutiques go beyond typical souvenirs, presenting carefully curated collections made by local craftsmen. These shops emphasize quality and authenticity, offering products that tell a story. Handmade leather goods, olive wood kitchenware, and hand-carved figurines echo the skills and passions of the artisans behind them.

Walking into one of these boutiques, you can often meet the creators themselves or hear tales about the origins of their craft. This personal connection turns shopping into a meaningful cultural exchange, allowing visitors to bring home more than just an object but a piece of Athens' soul.

Fashion Districts and Designer Stores

For those drawn to fashion and contemporary style, Athens presents an exciting contrast to its ancient surroundings. The city's fashion districts pulse with creativity, showcasing both established Greek designers and emerging talents. In areas like Kolonaki, chic boutiques sit alongside international brands, creating a stylish hub where classic elegance meets avant-garde trends.

Kolonaki's streets are lined with sleek stores featuring carefully designed clothing, footwear, and accessories that appeal to discerning shoppers. Here, you can discover everything from high-end fashion labels to concept stores that highlight sustainable and ethical designs, reflecting Greece's growing influence in the global fashion scene.

Adjacent neighborhoods also offer a variety of designer stores where you can find limited-edition pieces and innovative styles. Shopping in these districts is not just about purchasing but also about experiencing Athens' evolving fashion identity—a blend of Mediterranean flair, modern minimalism, and bold creativity.

Flea Markets and Vintage Finds

For a more eclectic shopping adventure, Athens' flea markets provide a vibrant and colorful atmosphere full of surprises. The most famous among them is the Monastiraki Flea Market, a labyrinth of stalls and shops where antiques, second-hand goods, and quirky collectibles await discovery.

Monastiraki Flea Market

SCAN THE QR CODE

- Open your phone's camera app
- Most smartphones have a built-in QR scanner in the camera.
- Point the camera at the QR code
- Make sure the code is clear and within the frame.
- Wait for the notification
- A link or message should pop up on your screen.
- Tap the notification
- This will open the link or content in your browser or a relevant app.
- Follow the instructions on the screen
- You will be taken to a Google Maps, app where you can now click on your current location to get to your destination.

Here, the air is thick with excitement as vendors haggle with customers, each stall offering a glimpse into different eras and styles. Vintage clothing, retro jewelry, old books, vinyl records, and even rare memorabilia are among the treasures that attract locals and tourists alike.

Exploring the market requires patience and curiosity—sometimes the best finds are hidden in unexpected corners. Beyond the tangible goods, the lively environment itself—with street performers, local cafes, and the backdrop of the ancient Agora—makes the flea market a unique cultural experience.

Other flea markets and vintage shops scattered throughout the city cater to those with a taste for nostalgia and originality, offering everything from classic designer pieces to handmade crafts that fuse old and new aesthetics.

Specialty Shops: Olive Oil, Honey, and Local Crafts

No visit to Athens would be complete without indulging in the city's culinary and artisanal specialties, and the many specialty shops dedicated to these treasures offer a feast for the senses. Olive oil, regarded as liquid gold in Greece, is featured prominently in shops where you can sample and purchase some of the finest varieties, often cold-pressed and sourced from family-owned groves.

Honey, another prized product, comes in numerous regional varieties—thyme, pine, and wildflower among them—each with its own distinct flavor and aroma. Specialty stores provide an opportunity to learn about the beekeeping traditions that have thrived for centuries and to select pure, artisanal honey that is both a delicious treat and a healthful gift.

Local crafts also shine in these shops, showcasing textiles, pottery, and handmade goods that reflect Greece's diverse landscapes and cultural heritage. From embroidered linens to painted ceramics and intricate jewelry, these products carry the imprint of ancient traditions combined with modern craftsmanship.

Shopping for these items often includes a personal touch, with shopkeepers eager to share stories about the origins of their products and the communities that produce them. This knowledge adds depth to every purchase, turning shopping into an immersive experience that connects visitors with the land and its people.

Outdoor and Recreational Activities

Athens is often celebrated for its rich history and bustling urban life, but it's also a city that invites exploration of its natural landscapes and outdoor experiences. Whether you seek panoramic views from hilltops, sun-soaked beaches, serene parks, or charming day trips beyond the city limits, Athens offers a refreshing blend of recreation and relaxation that complements its cultural treasures. This chapter opens the door to the outdoor pursuits that can deepen your connection with the city's environment and lifestyle.

Hiking Trails: Mount Lycabettus and Philopappos Hill

One of the most rewarding ways to engage with Athens is on foot, particularly by hiking its prominent hills that offer breathtaking vistas and a chance to escape the urban buzz. Mount Lycabettus stands as the city's highest point, rising dramatically over the skyline. The ascent is a favorite among locals and visitors alike, a moderately challenging hike through pine-scented paths that culminates in spectacular views stretching from the Acropolis to the distant Saronic Gulf.

The summit of Lycabettus reveals Athens in a way no other vantage point can. From here, the city sprawls endlessly, a tapestry of ancient monuments, bustling neighborhoods, and shimmering coastline. The chapel of St. George at the top adds a historical touch, and the café there invites hikers to rest and savor the panorama with a refreshing drink.

Nearby, Philopappos Hill offers a gentler climb but no less enchanting experience. Named after the Roman prince who built a monument on its peak, this hill is dotted with ancient ruins and shaded by olive and cypress trees. Walking its winding paths feels like stepping into a living painting, where history and nature entwine. The hill's terraces provide quiet spots to pause and absorb views of the Acropolis, the city's rooftops, and the sea beyond.

Both hills are excellent spots for sunrise or sunset hikes. The soft morning light bathes Athens in golden hues, while evenings here glow with the city's lights coming alive beneath the stars. For many, these hikes become memorable rituals—a way to witness Athens' beauty in its most natural and serene form.

Beaches along the Athens Riviera

Though Athens is famous for its archaeological marvels, it's also blessed with a coastline that stretches along the Athenian Riviera, where azure waters and sandy shores invite a leisurely escape. A short trip from the city center leads to an array of beaches catering to different moods and preferences.

Glyfada, one of the most popular seaside suburbs, combines lively beach clubs with tranquil stretches of sand. Here, visitors can lounge under umbrellas, take refreshing dips, or enjoy waterfront dining that blends fresh seafood with spectacular views. The area buzzes with energy in summer, with locals and tourists alike embracing the sun and sea.

Further south, beaches like Vouliagmeni and Varkiza offer more peaceful settings. Vouliagmeni, famous for its natural thermal lake, combines therapeutic waters with a beautiful beachfront. The lake's mineral-rich waters are known to soothe muscles and refresh the spirit, making it a unique spot for wellness seekers.

Vouliagmeni Beach

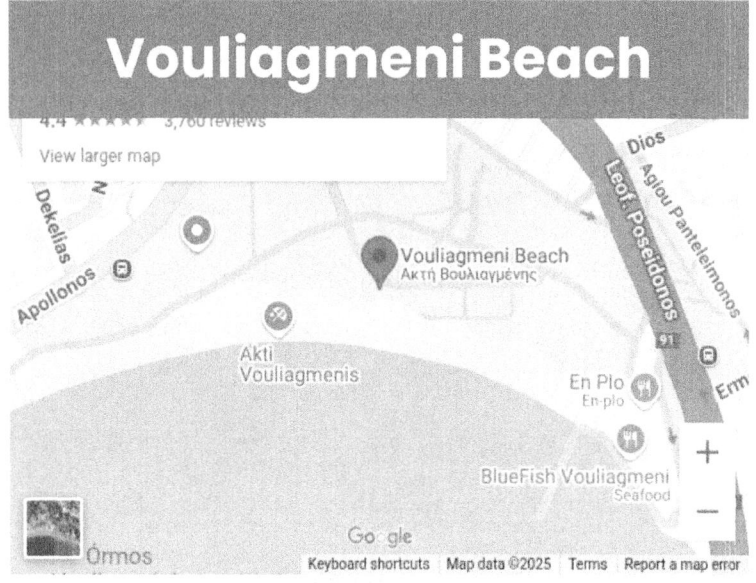

4.4 ★★★★★ 3,760 reviews

View larger map

SCAN THE QR CODE

- Open your phone's camera app
- Most smartphones have a built-in QR scanner in the camera.
- Point the camera at the QR code
- Make sure the code is clear and within the frame.
- Wait for the notification
- A link or message should pop up on your screen.
- Tap the notification
- This will open the link or content in your browser or a relevant app.
- Follow the instructions on the screen
- You will be taken to a Google Maps, app where you can now click on your current location to get to your destination.

Varkiza's wide, sandy beach is family-friendly, with calm waters and facilities that cater to a relaxed day by the sea. Smaller, hidden coves dot the coastline between these popular beaches, perfect for those who want to avoid crowds and find a quiet spot to swim and unwind.

The Riviera's beaches are not just for sunbathing. They offer opportunities for water sports like windsurfing, paddleboarding, and sailing, allowing adventurous travelers to experience the sea actively while enjoying stunning views of the Attica coastline.

Parks and Green Spaces in the City

For those who prefer greenery within the city's heartbeat, Athens provides several parks and gardens that offer welcome respites from the urban rush. The National Garden, located just behind the Greek Parliament building, is a verdant oasis where ancient trees, fragrant flowers, and peaceful ponds create a cool retreat. Strolling through winding paths here, visitors can encounter turtles, exotic plants, and even a small botanical museum that adds educational charm.

Another notable green space is Pedion tou Areos, one of the largest public parks in Athens. This expansive area is a favorite for joggers, families, and picnickers. Statues and fountains scattered throughout the park pay homage to Greek history and culture, enriching the environment with artistic significance.

Zappeion Garden, near the entrance to the National Garden, combines manicured lawns with neoclassical architecture and fountains, making it a perfect spot to relax or enjoy a book under the shade. Its proximity to the Acropolis also makes it a convenient stop on a day of sightseeing.

For a more contemporary take on green space, Technopolis in Gazi blends an industrial heritage site with open areas for events, markets, and festivals. It often hosts outdoor concerts and cultural happenings, turning green areas into lively community hubs.

These parks invite visitors to slow down, breathe deeply, and appreciate Athens' ability to balance urban life with natural beauty.

Day Trips to Nearby Islands and Coastal Towns

While Athens itself captivates with its combination of history and modernity, its location makes it an excellent base for memorable day trips to islands and coastal towns. The city's proximity to the Saronic Gulf offers easy access to charming destinations that feel worlds away from the capital's bustling streets.

The island of Aegina is a favorite for a quick getaway, reachable by a short ferry ride from Piraeus port. Known for its pistachio groves and friendly atmosphere, Aegina invites visitors to wander through quaint villages, swim in crystal-clear waters, and sample fresh seafood at waterfront taverns.

Hydra, another accessible island, is famed for its preserved architecture and ban on motor vehicles, creating a serene environment where donkeys and boats replace cars. This island's artistic legacy and picturesque harbor make it a delightful place to explore on foot or by boat.

Closer to the mainland, the coastal town of Vouliagmeni boasts a beautiful lake and beach, blending natural wonders with luxurious resorts and spas. It offers both relaxation and adventure, from swimming in thermal waters to hiking nearby trails.

For those eager to explore ancient history alongside scenic beauty, the town of Nafplio lies a bit further but remains a feasible day trip. Its Venetian fortress, narrow streets, and seaside charm provide a perfect blend of culture and leisure.

Whether you seek the calm of island life or the quaintness of coastal towns, these excursions offer a refreshing complement to your Athens experience, letting you immerse in Greece's diverse landscapes and traditions.

Practical Travel Tips for Athens

Traveling to Athens can be an exhilarating experience, filled with the promise of ancient wonders, vibrant neighborhoods, and Mediterranean charm. Yet, to truly enjoy everything this city has to offer, a little preparation goes a long way. Understanding practical matters such as currency, language, safety, health, and even the best times to visit will help you navigate Athens confidently and comfortably. This section offers essential advice and insider knowledge to ensure your trip runs smoothly from start to finish.

Currency, Tipping, and Budgeting

When it comes to handling money in Athens, the currency used is the euro (€), which is the standard across most of Europe. ATMs are widespread and easily accessible in the city center, airports, and major tourist areas, allowing visitors to withdraw cash as needed. Credit and debit cards are also widely accepted in hotels, restaurants, shops, and even many taxis, although it's wise to carry some cash for smaller vendors, street markets, or traditional tavernas that may prefer it.

Tipping in Athens is generally appreciated but not mandatory. In restaurants, it's customary to leave around 5 to 10 percent of the bill if service was good, though rounding up the amount or leaving some small change is perfectly acceptable in casual eateries. For taxi drivers, rounding up the fare or adding a euro or two is standard practice. Hotel staff, such as bellhops or housekeeping, often receive small tips as a gesture of gratitude, but there is no strict rule.

Budgeting for your trip will depend on your style of travel. Athens caters to a broad spectrum, from budget backpackers to luxury travelers. Affordable meals can be found in local markets and casual tavernas where hearty portions of Greek classics won't break the bank. Museums and archaeological sites typically charge moderate entrance fees, with discounts available for students, seniors, and families. Public transport is economical and efficient, making it easy to explore without splurging on taxis or rental cars.

Planning ahead with a rough daily budget that includes accommodation, food, transportation, and entrance fees will help you stay on track while also allowing some flexibility for spontaneous experiences. Whether you're dining at a simple souvlaki stand or indulging in a rooftop dinner with views of the Acropolis, Athens offers options to suit every budget.

Language Basics and Communication

Greek is the official language of Athens, and its alphabet is distinct and beautiful, although it might look daunting at first glance. While many Athenians speak English, especially younger people and those working in tourism, learning a few basic Greek phrases can enrich your experience and open doors to friendlier interactions.

Simple greetings such as "Kalimera" (Good morning), "Efharisto" (Thank you), and "Parakaló" (Please/You're welcome) are appreciated and often met with warm smiles. Asking "Pos ise?" (How are you?) or "Pothé íste?" (Where are you from?) can spark pleasant conversations and show respect for the local culture.

Communication beyond language is often warm and welcoming. Greeks are known for their hospitality, and many locals will go out of their way to help travelers navigate the city or find hidden gems. Mobile connectivity is strong in Athens, and free Wi-Fi spots are common in cafés, museums, and public spaces, making it easy to stay connected or use navigation apps while on the go.

If you plan to visit less touristy neighborhoods or venture further afield, carrying a phrasebook app or translation tool can be handy, though it's worth remembering that gestures and a friendly attitude often transcend language barriers.

Safety Tips and Emergency Contacts

Athens is generally a safe city for travelers, with low levels of violent crime and a visible police presence, especially in tourist areas. Like in any major city, however, it's wise to stay alert to pickpockets and petty theft, particularly in crowded places such as markets, public transport, and busy squares. Keeping wallets and phones secure, avoiding displaying large amounts of cash, and using hotel safes for valuables are practical precautions.

Walking around neighborhoods in daylight is safe, but it's advisable to avoid poorly lit or deserted streets at night. When taking taxis, choosing official, metered cabs or using trusted ride-sharing apps reduces the risk of overcharging or unsafe experiences.

In case of emergencies, the European emergency number 112 works throughout Greece and connects callers to police, fire, or medical services. The local police can also be reached at 100, and ambulance services at 166. Many hotels and hostels provide emergency contact information and can assist travelers if needed.

Travel insurance is recommended to cover unexpected health issues, lost belongings, or trip cancellations. Athens has reliable emergency services and hospitals, but having insurance gives peace of mind and access to English-speaking assistance if necessary.

Health and Medical Facilities

Athens boasts a robust healthcare system with well-equipped hospitals, clinics, and pharmacies. For minor ailments or common travel inconveniences such as sunburn or allergies, local pharmacies ("farmakeia") are plentiful and often staffed by knowledgeable pharmacists who can recommend over-the-counter remedies.

Major hospitals in the city have emergency rooms and specialists available, and many doctors speak English. It's advisable to carry any prescription medications you need, along with their generic names, as some brands may differ in Greece. Vaccinations required for Greece are generally routine; however, it's a good idea to be up to date on standard immunizations such as tetanus.

Heat in the summer can be intense, so staying hydrated and protecting yourself from the sun is essential. Athens also experiences occasional bursts of Saharan dust, which may affect those with respiratory conditions. If you have specific health concerns, consulting with your healthcare provider before travel is wise.

For travelers with allergies or dietary restrictions, Greek cuisine is generally accommodating, but it's helpful to learn key phrases to communicate your needs in restaurants or shops.

Seasonal Weather and What to Pack

Athens enjoys a Mediterranean climate characterized by hot, dry summers and mild, wet winters. The best time to visit largely depends on your preferences for weather, crowds, and activities.

Spring (April to June) and autumn (September to October) offer pleasant temperatures, abundant sunshine, and fewer tourists, making them ideal for sightseeing and outdoor activities. During these months, daytime temperatures generally range from the mid-60s to the mid-80s Fahrenheit (around 18 to 30 degrees Celsius), with comfortable evenings.

Summer (July and August) is the peak tourist season, drawing visitors eager to experience the city's vibrant energy and nearby beaches. However, temperatures can soar into the 90s and even higher (mid-30s Celsius), so packing light, breathable clothing, sunblock, sunglasses, and a hat is essential. Many locals take their holidays during August, so some businesses may close, but tourist sites remain open.

Winter (November to March) is mild but wetter, with temperatures typically between the mid-40s and mid-60s Fahrenheit (7 to 18 degrees Celsius). While Athens rarely sees snow, occasional chilly winds mean a warm jacket is advisable. This season offers a quieter, more local experience and lower accommodation rates.

No matter the season, comfortable walking shoes are a must. Athens' cobblestone streets, archaeological sites, and uneven pavements require sturdy footwear. A small daypack, reusable water bottle, and a portable charger for your devices will keep you well-prepared for full days of exploration.

Athens for Special Interests

Athens is a city that captivates a wide range of travelers, offering something unique and memorable for every kind of visitor. Beyond the well-trodden paths of ancient ruins and bustling markets, the city embraces special interests that make it not just a destination but an experience tailored to diverse lifestyles and passions. Whether you're traveling with family, identifying with the LGBTQ+ community, working remotely as a digital nomad, or seeking eco-conscious adventures, Athens provides welcoming spaces, vibrant events, and thoughtful options to enrich your journey.

Family-Friendly Activities and Attractions

Traveling to Athens with children can be a wonderful experience, filled with opportunities to blend education and fun in an environment that's both safe and stimulating. The city has made significant strides in becoming family-friendly, with attractions, parks, and activities that captivate younger visitors while providing parents with peace of mind.

One of the highlights for families is the interactive and engaging museums scattered throughout Athens. The Hellenic Children's Museum, located in the Plaka district, offers hands-on exhibits that encourage creativity and learning through play. It's a space designed to inspire curiosity in young minds, providing activities that touch on Greek culture, art, and science. Similarly, the Goulandris Natural History Museum allows children to explore biodiversity through colorful displays of fossils, animals, and ecosystems, making science exciting and accessible.

Parks and open spaces are crucial for families on the move, and Athens delivers on this front as well. The National Garden, situated near the Parliament building, is an oasis of greenery where children can run freely, feed ducks, or enjoy the small playground. Pedion tou Areos, another vast park, offers large green areas, fountains, and walking paths ideal for family picnics and leisurely strolls. Both provide a welcome break from urban bustle and a safe environment for kids to explore nature.

Historic sites are also more approachable for families when mixed with storytelling and engaging tours. Many guided tours tailored to children are available, transforming monuments like the Acropolis or the Ancient Agora into exciting adventures where stories of gods, heroes, and philosophers come alive. These tours are designed to maintain attention and spark imaginations, ensuring that visits are enjoyable and educational.

Dining with children is another area where Athens shines. Traditional tavernas and casual eateries across the city are generally very welcoming to families, often offering kid-friendly menus and accommodating requests. Many restaurants feature outdoor seating, which provides a relaxed atmosphere where children can be comfortable and parents can savor authentic Greek flavors without stress.

LGBTQ+ Friendly Spaces and Events

Athens has steadily grown into one of Europe's most welcoming capitals for LGBTQ+ travelers, celebrated for its vibrant queer culture and inclusive atmosphere. The city boasts a range of spaces—from laid-back cafés and bars to dynamic clubs—that offer safe environments where diversity is celebrated openly.

Neighborhoods like Gazi stand out as hubs of LGBTQ+ nightlife and socializing. Here, visitors can find everything from lively dance clubs hosting themed parties to cozy bars where locals and tourists mingle freely. The scene is welcoming, with an emphasis on freedom of expression and community support.

Annual events such as Athens Pride further underscore the city's commitment to inclusivity. This colorful, joyous celebration usually takes place in June and features a parade through the city center, performances, and parties. It's a time when the city pulses with energy, and visitors can feel the warmth and solidarity of the local LGBTQ+ community.

Beyond nightlife and events, Athens offers cultural venues that explore queer themes and histories. Independent theaters, film festivals, and art galleries regularly showcase works that reflect LGBTQ+ experiences, adding depth and dimension to the city's cultural fabric.

Accommodations with a focus on inclusivity are also available, with many boutique hotels and guesthouses openly welcoming LGBTQ+ guests. These places often provide tailored information about friendly venues and events, helping visitors connect with the community and enjoy a truly affirming stay.

Digital Nomads: Work-Friendly Spots and Connectivity

For those who blend travel with remote work, Athens is emerging as a compelling destination. The city's rich history, combined with its affordable living costs compared to other European capitals, make it an attractive base for digital nomads seeking inspiration alongside productivity.

Athens offers a variety of coworking spaces scattered across neighborhoods such as Koukaki, Monastiraki, and Kolonaki. These hubs are designed with flexible memberships, high-speed internet, and comfortable work environments. Many incorporate cafés or communal kitchens, encouraging networking and collaboration among freelancers, entrepreneurs, and creatives.

Cafés, a staple of Athenian social life, also double as excellent remote work spots. Establishments with reliable Wi-Fi, ample seating, and a welcoming atmosphere abound. Some even feature power outlets and quiet corners ideal for deep focus. The city's thriving coffee culture ensures that good espresso or a refreshing iced frappe is always within reach during long work sessions.

Connectivity in Athens is reliable, with widespread 4G coverage and increasing availability of 5G in the central districts. Public libraries and some cultural centers also provide free Wi-Fi, allowing for varied environments depending on one's work style.

Aside from practical workspaces, Athens offers digital nomads the chance to balance work with leisure. Weekends can be spent exploring archaeological sites, hiking nearby hills, or enjoying vibrant street life. This balance between work and play is part of the city's growing appeal as a destination where professional needs and personal interests can coexist harmoniously.

Sustainable and Eco-Friendly Travel Options

As awareness of environmental issues grows worldwide, Athens is making strides toward sustainable tourism and eco-friendly travel experiences. Visitors who prioritize green practices will find many opportunities to minimize their footprint while still enjoying the city's wonders.

Public transportation is an excellent way to travel sustainably within Athens. The metro system is modern, efficient, and connects key areas including the airport, city center, and coastal neighborhoods. Buses and trams complement the network, offering affordable and eco-friendly alternatives to taxis or rental cars. Additionally, bike-sharing programs and electric scooters have become increasingly popular, providing flexible and green ways to navigate the city.

Several tour operators now focus on sustainable experiences, such as walking tours that highlight Athens' natural and cultural heritage without relying on motorized transport. These tours often include visits to lesser-known neighborhoods or green spaces, allowing travelers to discover a different side of the city while respecting local environments.

For eco-conscious diners, many restaurants and cafés emphasize organic, locally sourced ingredients, and vegetarian or vegan menus. The city's growing interest in farm-to-table dining supports local farmers and reduces food miles, aligning with sustainability values.

Athens also features parks and community gardens maintained with environmental stewardship in mind. Spaces like the National Garden not only offer recreation but also serve as urban green lungs, contributing to biodiversity and cleaner air in the bustling metropolis.

Visitors interested in sustainable shopping can explore markets and shops that prioritize handmade, locally produced goods, such as olive oil, honey, and ceramics crafted with traditional methods. Supporting these artisans helps preserve cultural heritage and promotes responsible consumption.

Lastly, Athens hosts events and initiatives dedicated to environmental awareness and sustainability. Throughout the year, conferences, workshops, and community clean-up days invite both locals and travelers to participate in making the city greener and more livable.

Conclusion and Final Thoughts

Athens stands today as a city where the threads of ancient history and modern vibrancy weave together seamlessly, creating a rich and multi-layered tapestry of experiences. By 2025, this dynamic capital continues to captivate visitors not only through its iconic archaeological treasures but also through its thriving cultural scene, innovative cuisine, and warm, welcoming spirit. The city's ability to evolve while honoring its roots is what makes Athens truly unique—a place where past and present converse in a way that enchants every traveler, regardless of their interests or background.

Reflecting on the journey through Athens, one can appreciate how the city's allure extends far beyond its well-known landmarks. The Acropolis and Parthenon still inspire awe, as symbols of a civilization that shaped Western thought and art, but the city's story is enriched by vibrant neighborhoods like Plaka and Monastiraki, where tradition hums alongside contemporary life. The bustling markets, the museums brimming with treasures, the local tavernas serving dishes passed down through generations, and the buzzing nightlife paint a picture of a city that is as alive today as it was millennia ago.

Athens in 2025 is more than just a destination for sightseeing—it is a place that invites authentic encounters. The charm lies in the small details: a friendly conversation with a vendor at Varvakios Market, the unexpected discovery of street art in Psyrri, or a sunset viewed from the quiet heights of Mount Lycabettus. These moments offer a deeper connection to the city's soul and its people. They remind visitors that travel is not only about checking off famous sites but also about immersing oneself in the rhythms of daily life, appreciating local customs, and understanding the layers that make a city alive.

As you consider your own journey to Athens, it's important to approach the city with respect and openness. This means honoring the cultural heritage that the Athenians are proud of, being mindful of the impact tourism can have on historical sites, and engaging thoughtfully with the communities you encounter. Sustainable and responsible travel practices—such as using public transportation, supporting local artisans, and minimizing waste—help ensure that Athens remains vibrant and accessible for generations to come.

The local people of Athens are, above all, proud hosts. Their hospitality is genuine, and many will go out of their way to share stories, recommend hidden gems, or simply welcome visitors with warmth. Taking the time to learn a few basic Greek phrases, respecting local customs, and showing appreciation for their culture can open doors to memorable interactions that transform a simple visit into a meaningful experience.

For those looking to plan their trip, a variety of resources are available to help make the experience as smooth and rewarding as possible.

Official tourism websites offer up-to-date information on events, transportation, and practical advice. Numerous guidebooks and travel apps provide detailed maps, insider tips, and curated itineraries tailored to different interests—whether you're focused on history, food, or the arts. Local tour operators, many of whom specialize in small group or private tours, offer personalized experiences that go beyond the typical tourist paths.

Emergency contacts, embassy information, and health facilities are also essential resources that travelers should keep handy. Athens is a safe city overall, but being prepared helps provide peace of mind. Tourist information centers, often staffed by multilingual personnel, are scattered throughout the city and serve as invaluable points of assistance, ready to answer questions and provide guidance.

Ultimately, Athens invites you to become part of its ongoing story. It is a city that rewards curiosity, embraces diversity, and thrives on connections between people from all walks of life. Whether you wander through the ancient ruins, savor the evolving flavors of Greek cuisine, or simply sit with a coffee watching the world go by in a neighborhood square, you are stepping into a living mosaic of culture and history.

This personal invitation to experience Athens is also an invitation to pause, reflect, and celebrate the joys of discovery. It encourages travelers to engage with the city on their own terms—whether that means exploring the archaeological wonders with scholarly interest, enjoying the pulse of contemporary arts, or simply basking in the Mediterranean sun by the sea.

Printed in Dunstable, United Kingdom

74520382R00067